THE

GHOSTLY TALES

OF

ELLICOTT CITY

Published by Arcadia Children's Books
A Division of Arcadia Publishing
Charleston, SC
www.arcadiapublishing.com

Spooky America is a trademark of Arcadia Publishing, Inc.

First published 2022

Manufactured in the United States

ISBN 978-1-4671-9831-8

Library of Congress Control Number: 2022933031

Alli mages used courtesy of Shutterstock.com; p. 56 loc.gov.

Notice: The information in this book is true and complete to the best of our knowledge. It is offered without guarantee on the part of the author or Arcadia Publishing. The author and Arcadia Publishing disclaim all liability in connection with the use of this book.

Spooky America

THE GHOSTLY TALES OF ELLICOTT CITY

DEBORAH MORGENTHAL

Adapted from *Haunted Ellicott City* by Shelley Davies Wygant

arcadia
CHILDREN'S BOOKS

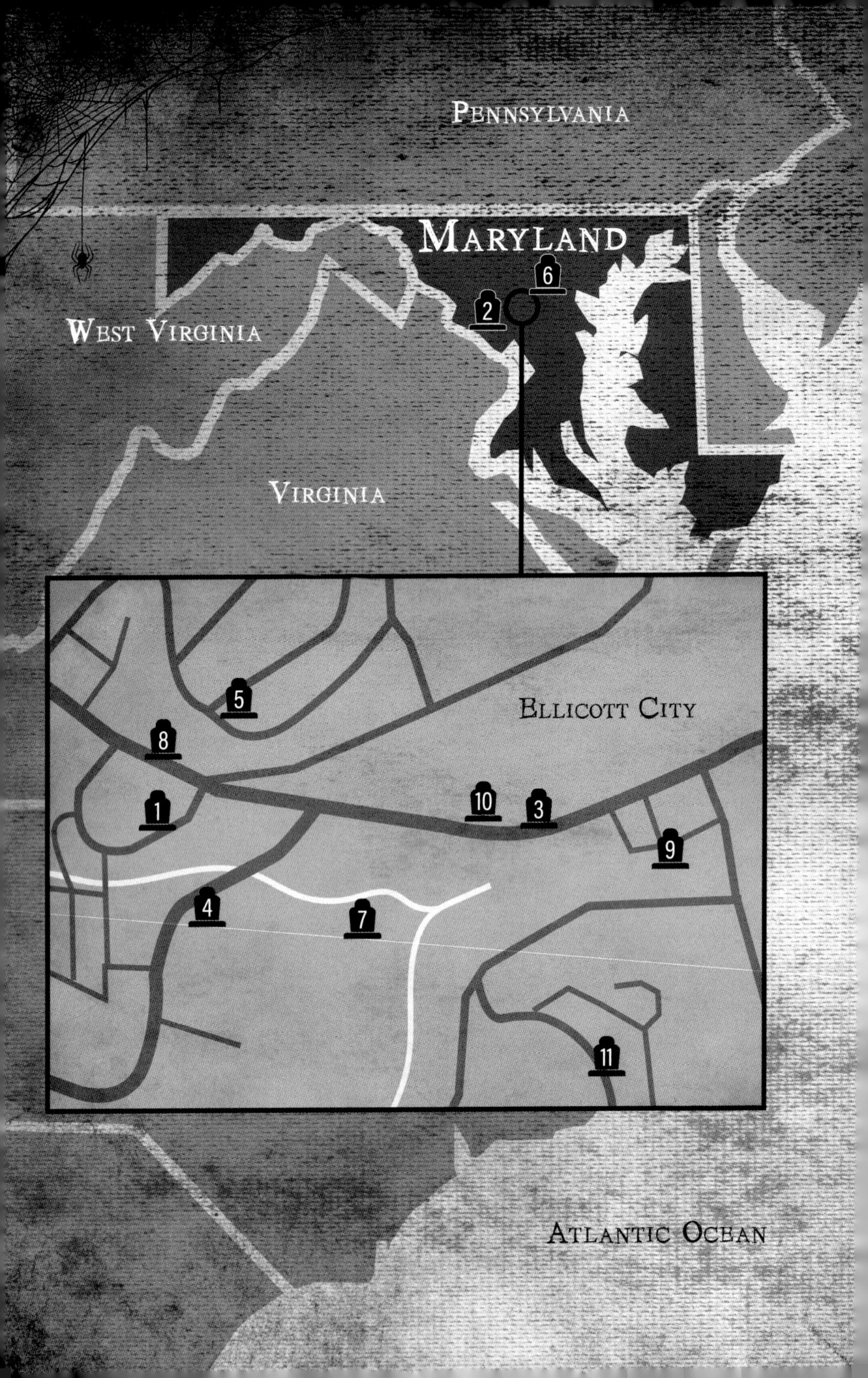
Pennsylvania
Maryland
West Virginia
Virginia
Ellicott City
Atlantic Ocean
1
2
3
4
5
6
7
8
9
10
11

TABLE OF CONTENTS & MAP KEY

Introduction

Welcome to Ellicott City, just fourteen miles from Baltimore, Maryland—home to many, many ghosts. Some paranormal experts say it's the most haunted town in America. The small city sits in a narrow granite ravine that was carved out by thousands of years of water from the Tiber Branch flowing down to the Patapsco River.

Why are so many ghosts attracted to Ellicott City? One explanation is that the coarse rock of the area holds a powerful electrical charge that can store and then release experiences from the past, such as important historical events, including the Civil War. Then there's all that moving water, thought to be catnip to beings from the spirit world. After you read the spooky stories in this book, maybe you'll be convinced that Ellicott City is a "thin place"—meaning that spirits can easily travel back and forth from the alive world to the one beyond.

All that water is what drew three Quaker brothers, Joseph, Andrew, and John, from Bucks County, Pennsylvania, to this 325-acre piece of wilderness in 1772. After cutting a six-mile wilderness road up river, the Ellicotts developed a sawmill, a granite quarry, a gristmill to grind wheat and other grains, several farms, and a small village. The power from the water, plus the rich soil, was just what they needed to make their mill—and the town they founded—a success. No wonder the town was first called Ellicott Mills!

All that water also had a dangerous side: Since 1780, the town has been nearly swept away by a dozen serious floods. Fortunately, no one was killed in that first flood, but eighty-eight years later, on July 24, 1868, nearly forty people living near the mill died in a terrible flood. In recent years, hurricanes caused more tragedies. The Hurricane Agnes flood of 1972 and the flash floods of 2016 and 2018 caused more death and destruction. The 2018 flood destroyed the town a second time. And then there's fire . . . Ellicott City has dealt with several fires that burned or damaged many of the town's buildings. Do you think that the destruction from water and fire explains why the city boasts so many nice and not-so-nice spirits from the other side?

Or are the trains that pass through the city the reason for all that ghost travel? Over more than 200 years, thousands of living passengers have come through the Baltimore & Ohio Railroad Station at Ellicott's Mills on their way to the city or points west. Completed in 1831, the two-story, granite B&O Railroad Station building at 3711 Maryland Avenue is the first and oldest commercial railroad station terminus in the United States. It was built as the ending point for the first thirteen miles of commercial railroad track that ran between Baltimore and Ellicott's Mills. Perhaps the town was the true last stop for many of these people. And then their spirits decided to unpack and never leave.

Whatever the reasons, the town is so popular with ghosts that there are special tours that offer visitors the chance to meet and greet some of these spectral residents. As you'll discover when you dig into this collection of 13 spooky stories, some are friendly—some, not so much. Some, like the spirit firefighters, are still on duty. Others, like the very scary tunnel ghost, will make you run the other way. How to explain the silent blue orbs that folks describe in many downtown stores? The mysterious noises heard in the dark of night? We may never know for sure why so many ghosts make their home in this Maryland city.

Are you ready for your personal tour of the most haunted town in America? Then come on along as we meet these doomed souls. Be warned: a few of them may want you to be their friends . . . forever!

Welcome, One and All, Alive . . . and Dead

The stone building that houses the Howard County Welcome Center at 8267 Main Street used to be a post office. But before the time when people came to send and receive mail, the site was home to a place where there was no forwarding address: people had relocated . . . from life . . . to the afterlife. You see, a funeral home was located on that site for many years, which might explain why visitors and employees at the Welcome Center hear strange sounds, see weird sights, and breathe in the overly sweet smell of flowers.

Perched at the top of Main Street, the large stone building was originally constructed on land where several homes stood in 1839. A few decades later, those residences were replaced in part by the W.J. Bewley Funeral Home on Main Street, with Gaither Livery Stables around back. William James Bewley and his older brother Lemuel ran the funeral home for a number of years until William's death in 1872.

The following year, Stephen Jones Hillsinger purchased the building and the undertaking business. There is always a need for funeral homes, so it's no surprise that Hillsinger Undertaking Parlor lasted for many years, as did its owner. In

1920, two years before he died on Halloween night at the age of eighty-one, Hillsinger was still listed as working as an undertaker.

In 1937, the funeral home and the livery were torn down to make room for a new post office. When it was finished in 1940, the attractive one-story stone structure consisted of a public lobby with five windows for customers, an alcove with two hundred lockboxes, the postmaster's office, and a large workroom.

For nearly sixty years, residents of Ellicott City sent and received mail there, until a new post office was built near Route 40. Howard County purchased the old post office building in 2008 and turned the basement into the Howard County Welcome Center. In 2011, Howard County Tourism, Inc. moved upstairs. The basement offices are now home to the Howard County Police Museum. Although the building was closed for repairs after the floods of 2016 and 2018, it was not damaged. Today, it welcomes visitors and Ellicott City residents who are interested in learning about what's going on in the area. And perhaps after their visit, they will have learned a thing or two about ghostly happenings.

Employees and tourists frequently share stories about the mysterious sights, sounds, and smells they experience while at the Welcome Center. Often, they describe seeing a young woman who they agree desperately wants to be acknowledged and called by her rightful name.

In 2004, when the center was still the Ellicott City Post Office and the tourism offices were in the basement, a staff member heard something heavy being dragged across the floor above her. At first, she thought it was another post office employee pushing a crate into the mailroom. Then, with a tingle of fear, she remembered that the post office had closed hours earlier. How then to explain what she heard?

Others describe a rattling sound, as if someone is trying to open the storage room's doors. The sound stops before they can check it out. Then, just as soon as they return to their desks, they hear a thumping noise like a heartbeat coming from the empty room they just left. Once, staff members unlocked the door to the copy room and were shocked to see that a set of shelves that had been bolted to the wall at one end of the room was now located at the other end, with every item still in place. How weird is that?

One employee reported hearing what she was sure was the tap, tap, tap of high-heeled shoes clicking on hardwood floors—although the hall was carpeted. That would get your attention. This same staffer didn't believe her coworkers' ghost stories "until one day I was sitting in the back room talking to a coworker, gossiping, and I heard and felt someone lean in [to my left ear] and shush me and honestly, I got chills."

In addition to these odd sounds, there are particular smells that indicate that something supernatural is present. If you've ever been inside a funeral home or attended a funeral, perhaps you remember the strong smell of fresh flowers. Even with all the doors and windows open, staff and visitors to the Welcome Center say the strong aroma of flowers fills the back hall and the conference room. Some even tell the tour guides that the office smells like a funeral home.

It was Ed Lilley, the Center's manager and a longtime resident of Ellicott City, who was the one to meet the ghost when she finally showed herself. This occurred after the post office closed and the tourism office had moved to the main floor of the building. Ed spied the spirit one night when he was working late. He was sitting behind a desk near the ticket counter when he suddenly felt he was not alone. He sensed that someone was standing right in front of him.

Startled, he looked up and saw her. Although the vision lasted only a few seconds, his description was detailed. Standing at the end of the brochure rack was a woman in her mid-thirties. Her long brown hair flowed down around the shoulders of her white dress with its high, standup collar. Almost as soon as he saw her, the woman vanished—but not for good.

When Ed shared his experience with other staff members, he wasn't surprised to learn that many of them had also felt or seen the ghost woman's presence; one person reported she'd seen the young woman walking through the back hall of the office. Others said they felt a strange cold spot near the ticket counter.

The staff decided the spirit needed a name. Sometimes when we name a fear, it stops having the power to scare us. As soon as the employees began calling out their suggestions, the lights in the center began to flicker. Fearlessly, they continue their name search, which was interrupted when the phone on the front desk rang. Can you guess? When Ed answered, there was no one on the line. This seems to indicate the woman wanted them to reach a decision, so the group decided to call the ghost Caroline. Apparently, however, that name was not okay!

Over the next few days, the staff continued to hear strange noises, smell the too-sweet aroma of funeral home flowers, and sense the creepy presence of the spirit they had rushed to name. Perhaps you have a nickname that you dislike and find yourself correcting friends and family when they call you Mike, instead of Michael. Or maybe you've just never felt happy with the name your parents gave you. Was this dissatisfaction the source of the ghost's continued visitations?

One day, a visitor who came to buy a ticket for the town's ghost tour scheduled for later that evening received a glimpse of the "other side," and strongly felt that an invisible being was frantically trying to communicate with her. When the visitor returned to the Welcome Center that evening for the ghost tour, she told the tour guide what she'd experienced. She said the ghost wanted to let the staff know that her name wasn't Caroline but, rather, a name that began with the letter *L*. As the visitor considered her exchange with the spirit, she felt like the name was something like Loretta, Louise, or Louisa. From that day on, "Caroline" was replaced by the ghost known today as Louisa.

This apparition would not agree with Juliet, who, in William Shakespeare's famous play, *Romeo and Juliet*, famously said, "What's in a name? That which we call a rose. By any other name would smell as sweet." Basically, what it means is that what matters is what something is, not what it is called. But some ghosts appear to be VERY particular about being called by a certain name. Right, Louisa??

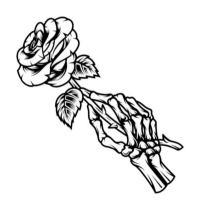

Fire Station Ghosts and One Loyal Dog

Apparently some spirits are homebodies (or ghostbodies!) who just can't leave a house they loved when they were alive. The same seems to be true for people who loved their jobs so much that even after their death they stay to complete work. Talk about dedication! In this spooky tale, it was a firehouse that drew together these two desires: never to leave the Station that was like home, and to stay in a job way, way after the workday had ended. This seems to be the case for several firefighters and their loyal dog at The Third Ellicott City Firehouse, also known as Station 2, located at 8390 Main Street.

One of the very first buildings visitors see when driving into town from the west is the Third Ellicott City Firehouse, constructed in the 1880s. Originally, the site featured the Charles T. Makinson Carriage Factory, building carriages for more than three decades. Near-tragedy struck on May 21, 1913, when a trolley conductor noticed flames shooting out of the back of the building. The Ellicott City Fire Company, then located at the Second Ellicott City Firehouse, just down the block at 8316 Main Street, arrived within minutes.

In spite of the quick response, the fire quickly spread to an adjoining grocery store where Nimrod Johnson and his wife and five children lived in an apartment above the shop. Fortunately, they all escaped unharmed.

Not so the buildings: Both structures and almost all of their contents were destroyed. Sadly, both shops were beyond repair and were torn down. Much of the property stayed vacant until 1937, when the Howard County Volunteer Fireman's Association bought "Lot 52" to build the Third Ellicott City Firehouse.

Completed in April 1939, the large building had a kitchen in the basement and an office and meeting rooms on the first floor. The second floor featured an apartment for Fire Chief Benjamin Harrison "Harry" Shipley Sr., his wife, "May," and his son Benjamin Harrison Jr., as well as a dorm and locker room for the men.

For the next sixty years, the Third Ellicott City Firehouse and its dedicated team of firefighters were prepared every day and night to tackle fires in the town and the surrounding area, until, in early 2000, the fire company moved to its current location on Montgomery Road.

Although there were deadly fires the men had to deal with over the years, nothing tragic happened at the old firehouse. But it's believed that the spirits of some of the people who died in fires over the course of sixty years may have hopped aboard a fire truck and hung out for eternity with the firemen who tried to save their life. Why do these stories continue to be told? Here's the 911: Over the years, when new firefighters and volunteers start working at Station 2, they report mysterious stuff, like the television in the men's dorm that often turns on by itself. Often, heavy chairs move across the floors, pushed by an invisible hand. When these stories are shared with the more experienced firefighters, they nod their heads knowingly. The new crew gradually comes to accept that some of their roommates are working a true "graveyard" shift!

Not all the living firemen can take the ghostly heat. One firefighter found the supernatural events to be too scary and would not stay in the firehouse alone. The crew would always find him outside the station when they returned from a fire.

Apparently, the spirits would wait until the firemen left, and then they would "go to work." Volunteers who stayed behind sometimes reported the sound of silverware clanging loudly from the kitchen located in the basement. Others heard the faint clacking of an old-fashioned typewriter in the office area above.

When the crew answered an alarm and no one was able to stay behind, the firemen would lock up the station, but when they returned, they found all the doors unlocked. This happened so often that they had all the locks changed in case someone had gotten hold of a key and was pranking them. But these ghosts were persistent. The new locks continued to open by themselves whenever the firefighters left the building.

Then there's the tale (or tail) about the fire station dog, Yogi. One Sunday afternoon while the firefighters were watching a football game, Yogi struck a pose of high alert—ears perked up, his eyes fixed on the door, seeming to follow the movements of someone or something walking through the door and down the hall toward the apartment where the long-dead Fire Chief Harrison Shipley Sr. and his family once lived.

At that point, Yogi raced down the hall and began to desperately bark and claw at the closed door. The men rushed after him and opened the door to the apartment. No one was there.

Some people believe that the eerie presences belong to the former fire chief, Harrison Shipley Sr., and his son, Harry Shipley Jr. Born in 1891, the senior Shipley, a former auto mechanic turned volunteer firefighter served and lived at Station 2 from 1935 to 1957 and died in 1967 at the age of seventy-six. In 2002, Harry Shipley Jr. passed away at the age of eighty-eight. Perhaps father and son delight in spooking their fellow firefighters ... all in good fun, of course!

On one occasion, the ghosts decided to appear in a more obvious way. Business owner Dave Carney reported that he once "captured a photo with four 'orbs,' so obviously, Shipley is not alone. I'm certain that one of the orbs was a former firehouse dog."

What do you think? Did Yogi finally catch up with his firefighter "person," who loved him so much? Wouldn't it be fun to play fetch with a ghost dog?

Mirror, Mirror, on the Wall . . .

Since the early 1800s, a three-part building complex that became known as Cacao Lane, has housed a number of businesses, and if you believe in these sorts of things, perhaps many supernatural guests and customers. Ghost experts explain that it takes time to build up the psychic energy that becomes a welcoming location for spirits from beyond to take root. First called the Alexander House, the building later housed two popular shops—Hunt's Dry Goods Store and Elizabeth Hunt's Ladies Millinery Shop. Located at 8066-8077 Main Street, the three interconnected stone structures were most recently the home of Cacao Lane Restaurant, which served Ellicott City diners for more than forty years. Many people believe that shoppers, bar hoppers, restaurant diners, and the staff who served them long ago have been replaced by lost souls who continue to spend time in this unusual building.

Restaurant employees share stores that are hard to forget. Some say they hear footsteps coming from the empty upstairs. Others

describe an apparition wearing a white shirt who wanders around the mezzanine. Still others report being frightened when empty bar stools suddenly spin around on their own. Are there ghost bartenders serving drinks—often called "spirits"— to, well, spirits?

One of the tales that keeps being told because it was so scary happened at Cacao Lane fairly recently, and some of those witnesses are still alive to share this frightening event.

Apparently right after the last guest left the restaurant, the servers were taking a break before closing up for the night. A group of them—including a few waiters, a cook, a dishwasher, and the bartender—were hanging out in the first-floor bar area relaxing after a long shift. The bartender—who had been looking out the large bay window at the now deserted Main Street—suddenly turned back to the group. As he did, something on the wall behind the bar caught his eye.

He managed to say out loud, "Hey, look" to his work friends, as he pointed to one of the large mirrors hanging on the brick wall. Then he silently froze. The rest of the group turned where he pointed just in time to see the mirror slowly rise straight up in the air by itself, leaving its hook on the wall. It surely would take your breath away to see something like that! But there's more!

You'd think the mirror would then fall to the floor and break, guaranteeing the witnesses years of bad luck. But that's not what happened. Instead of crashing to the floor, the mirror hovered above the shelves that held lots of bottles of "liquid spirits," as if it was being held in that mid-air position by an invisible hand. As the staff of stunned employees watched in amazed silence, the wire on the back of the frame caught the necks of a few bottles on the bottom row. The sound of the bottles crashing onto the floor broke the trance, and everyone ran out the front door.

The next morning, the mirror was found on the floor behind the bar. And here's the amazing part: The only broken glass was from the broken liquor bottles. The mirror itself was in one piece . . . not even a crack! How is that possible? It makes you wonder what would have happened if one of the employees had caught a glimpse of her own face in that supernatural mirror. Would her face have been changed into someone she wouldn't recognize? What if the

face of a ghost appeared in the looking glass instead of her own very alive face?

And here's the surprise ending to this most unusual story: the very next day, the restaurant manager simply rehung the mirror in its normal place on the wall behind the bar. Talk about business as usual! Customers continued to look in that spooky mirror for years to come. In fact, it never moved again until the devastating flood of 2016. That night, the powerful waters of a huge flash flood

crashed through the front windows of Cacao Lane and swept the haunted mirror into the Patapsco River, never to be seen again. Perhaps it sank to the bottom and has been enjoyed by ghoul fish and other mysterious water spirits. Do they look in the mirror and ask, "Who is the scariest of us all?"

Lady in White

Ghosts can appear anywhere at any time. Often they show up in buildings where people have died in violent ways, including being murdered. Perhaps their sudden deaths cause their spirits to stick close to the last place they were alive. Could this explain why the former livery stables known as Taylor's Row became a ghost hangout for one young woman wearing white petticoats?

The wood-sided buildings at 3733 Old Columbia Pike originally housed stables. Empty and abandoned for decades, Taylor's Row was renovated in the late 1990s and turned into a restaurant called the Mill Town Tavern, which was replaced by the Tiber River Tavern, and then by the Diamondback Tavern. In 2017, the roadside pub was sold yet again and become the home of the Manor Hill Tavern.

Early visitors to Ellicott City probably stabled their horses in Taylor's Row while they walked around the town. The original building consists of a series of stepped rooms with exposed stone walls. On the first floor there was a restaurant and kitchens. Two large dining rooms are upstairs, where bales of hay used to be stored. Other second-story rooms farther up the hill are used as office space. Visitors and tavern employees share stories about the many ghosts that hang around the place.

One spirit that shows up regularly is referred to as "Lady in White." During the 1920s, a woman was attacked and killed at the stable. A bartender who worked back when the place was called the Diamond Back Tavern recalled seeing her eerie presence more than three times. There used to be a long bar along the back wall of the large room to the right of the entrance. At the far-right end were double doors leading to the kitchen.

The bartender describes seeing the Lady in White for first time through the windows of that double door. She was standing at the end of the bar. The restaurant hadn't opened for customers yet, and he was concerned that someone had broken in, so he pushed through

the doors and started toward her. Suddenly, she turned to her left and walked toward the back hall that leads to the bathrooms. As he came around the corner, you guessed it, she vanished.

The second time, he only saw the white outline of her petticoats, but he knew it was the same silent ghost. He followed her again toward the bathrooms; as he came around the corner, she disappeared. The third time, he saw her in the lower-level main dining room, headed toward the bar area. I guess ghosts can get thirsty, too.

When the place was called the Tiber River Tavern, employees reported seeing bare footprints on the newly varnished floors. Along with seeing the Lady in White on many occasions, they also heard strange noises, distant voices, and muffled footsteps. Once, when they heard a loud crash overhead, the owner ran upstairs, unlocked the room, and found a table completely overturned. No one else was in the room!

Scared yet? Wait . . . there's more.

You'd expect to see the plates, glasses, and silverware scattered all over the floor, right? But, no. The place settings were perfectly in place underneath the overturned table.

Another longtime bartender admitted feeling uncomfortable talking about what he'd experienced. He said, "I hate the ghost and every time I talk about her something happens and, plus, I don't believe in it."

But then he agreed to tell his best story.

"It was a busy day," he began. "I was a barback then. I helped the bartenders clean up. It was the end of our shift, and the bartenders were all gone for the night. At that time, the tables in the lower-level dining room had white tablecloths and candles in the middle. During dinner service, we would light the candles and at the end of the night all had to be blown out before closing. Since I was the only one left downstairs, I blew out all the candles."

Then he said:

The general manager who was also a head bartender was upstairs, so I headed up to speak with him and let him know everyone was gone. He then came downstairs to check on things and started yelling for me to come back down and seemed upset. He said,

"What the heck! I thought you said you had closed up!"

"I did," I responded, and he said, "Well you better look again." So as I went into the dining room, all the tablecloths were lifted up in a bundle on the tables and I mean all the tables and one candle in the back was still lit. I was scared and just stared at the mess. The GM asked me again what had happened, I could not even answer, and I ran through the kitchen and out of this place.

Does the Lady in White mean anyone harm or is she just trying to get attention? Maybe she is lonely. Maybe she wants someone to help her solve the mystery of her murder. In any case, visitors to the Tavern today just might get to see a spirit from beyond to accompany the spirits they are drinking.

Don't Go Down into the Basement!

The Museum of Howard County History—home to a valuable collection of objects belonging to the county's most important families—dominates a hill over the city. When you visit, you can climb the hill to enjoy the programs presented by the Historical Society. You'll learn a lot of fascinating facts about the First Presbyterian Church once housed here, the former congregation, and perhaps, get an up-close glimpse of some ghostly members . . . if you're foolish enough to go into the basement!

Built in 1844, the front of the original church collapsed in 1893 during renovations to expand the building. As reported in the *Ellicott City Times*, the workmen who were excavating the basement: " . . . had partially completed their work when a suspicious noise was heard above and they left their work to make an investigation." Suddenly the entire front of the building came crashing down. Fortunately for the workmen, they were out of harm's way when the building collapsed or they would have been buried under the rubble. The congregation consulted with Baltimore architect George Archer, who recommended demolishing the remaining walls and building a new church on the site.

In its current life as a museum, the building boasts a basement in which many visitors report strange experiences. I don't know about you, but when I watch horror movies in which the lead character, threatened by scary beings— human or alien—opens the basement door to explore weird sounds, I want to shout: "Don't go into the basement!" Right? Unfortunately, until recently, the lower level was where the building's only bathroom was located. What's a person to do?? What would you do?

To reach the bathroom, you had to climb down a long flight of stairs into the murky and dank area beneath the sanctuary. You'd weave your way past an empty, dark office, and then through a maze of sheet-cloaked antique furniture and historic fixtures (which probably looked quite ghostly!) that were stored there. When you finally reached the tiny toilet area, you'd quickly turn on the light, close the door and lock it. When you were done, you'd bravely—and quickly—find your way back upstairs, sensing weird presences all around you, feeling relieved to be out of that spooky space and back in the light of the familiar.

What could explain these scary sensations? What could have gone so wrong in a church to result in sinister vibrations? Was the creepiness of the basement related to the funerals that were held there? Or is the source of doom and gloom related to the old Ellicott City Jail that was located a few steps away from the church? Built in 1878, the Ellicott City Jail had "dark cells" where condemned prisoners awaited their morning executions, horrific spectacles that attracted young and old alike. Is it possible that some of these wretched criminals sought refuge in the church basement after they died?

While it's anyone's guess who the spirits are, their existence is still being experienced, more than a hundred years later. Visitors to the museum report odd sounds rising up from the ceiling in the downstairs office. Volunteers report seeing objects mysteriously fall off the desks at which they're seated. Some people mention feeling gusts of freezing air chill their skin. Others say they hear the faint notes of a woman singing, her voice floating into the building from far away. However, not all the experiences are merely strange, but ultimately, harmless.

Some time ago, a museum manager who was rearranging items in the former lunchroom in the basement was attacked by an invisible something or someone. In fact, a paranormal investigator's camera recorded the deep scratch marks that were left on the manager's neck. I'm sure the marks left on this manager's memory are just as long lasting!

Fortunately, the bathroom was eventually moved to the museum's main floor. But some people, like in horror movies, just can't help looking for trouble! A few years after the bathroom had been relocated, a couple attending a concert decided to explore the basement, although the husband had doubts. In the past, he'd always felt nervous using the bathroom down there. Unfortunately, his wife enacted some version of "I dare you," and they cautiously descended the stairs into the gloomy basement. Suddenly, the husband stopped breathing and came to a sudden stop right next to the abandoned office that always seemed to be the center of psychic energy. Despite his wife egging him on, the husband stood his ground and insisted they leave. He firmly believed that someone was in that office: "And they *want* something."

Have you ever felt so scared that the hairs on the back of your neck stood up like the quills on a porcupine's back? That's what happened to this too-curious husband and wife. Quickly, they rushed up the stairs, no longer interested in being explorers of the underworld. Neither wanted to find out what the menacing spirit wanted from them.

Patapsco Female Institute

CHAPTER 6

The Very Homesick Ghost

The gigantic pile of stone perched on the highest hill above Ellicott City used to be the Patapsco Female Institute, a funny name for a girls' "finishing school," a boarding school for wealthy girls ages twelve to eighteen. Designed in the style called Greek Revival, the school was built in the 1830s at 3655 Church Road. In the more than hundred years since then, the building has had more lives than a cat.

It has been a hotel, a private home, a theater, a veteran's hospital, and now a historic county park. Thousands of people have been in and out of what was once a magnificent granite building or have visited the park. One unlucky girl seems to have never left.

There was a time when girls and boys were educated together in Ellicott City. As the town grew, local leaders decided to build an all-girls school on twelve acres of land and built the Patapsco Female Institute on that site in 1834. The fifty-seven-room school was large enough for eighty to one hundred students.

The Institute opened on January 1, 1837. Strange as this may seem to us now, back then many people believed that school for girls over the age of twelve was a bad thing. So it's all the more special that the school with the funny name offered girls the chance to study foreign languages, mathematics, music, religion, and philosophy. Way to go, Patapsco!

From 1841 to 1855, the school grew from six teachers and forty-one students to nine teachers and seventy students. Tuition for a twenty-two-week session covered "board," which means the room you slept in and the food you ate, plus "washing, use of bedding and other incidental expenses." Musical instruments, drawing and painting, and classes in Latin, Greek, French, Spanish, Italian, and German cost extra. Students who couldn't afford the full price could do chores to help them pay for school.

Most of the students came from the families of wealthy southern plantation owners, as well as from the families of politicians and other important business leaders in the South. For example, one student was Winnie Davis, the daughter of Jefferson Davis, the famous American politician who served as the president of the Confederate States from 1861 to 1865. Thomas Jefferson's great-granddaughter Sally Randolph served as the last headmistress of the school. As you know from studying American history, Thomas Jefferson was the third president of the United States from 1801 to 1809.

During the years since, the building has been bought and sold to different businesses, including an antique store and a summer resort hotel. Sadly, time has not been kind to the building; year after year more of its beauty has disappeared. When Howard County finally had the money to fix it up, it was no longer possible to return it to its original glory. What could be saved was saved, and the place became the Patapsco Female Institute Historic Park, which opened in 1995. In

2002, the Chesapeake Shakespeare Company started to perform plays there in the summer. Now people can rent the Park for weddings and can attend special events, such as a ghost tour that describes one unfortunate student who was dying to go home but never did.

Have you attended a boarding school? How about overnight camp? Sometimes spending time far from home can be lonely if you are not used to being away from your mom or dad. There may have been a lot of crying at night by girls who missed the life they were used to and the bed they usually slept in.

One sad girl was Annie Van Derlot. During her first semester at the school, she wrote home describing her time at school as her "incarceration," which is another word for captivity or imprisonment. How awful to feel that your school is a prison with no escape! There were a lot of rules at the Institute, and that may have made Annie's homesickness even worse.

In addition to feeling lonely, Annie may also have felt very cold! Although Maryland is not very far north, winters can be chilly. Girls used to the warm winters of South Carolina may have been unhappy with the weather and perhaps didn't bring enough warm clothes with them. In the winter months, many girls got sick with the flu, strep throat, and croup, which is a bad cold with a nasty cough. Yuck. Sick and lonely, they then spread their germs to others when they shared the chamber pots they used as toilets. Double yuck. One of the girls who caught the flu was our ghost-to-be, Annie. During her winter at the school, she caught a cold that got worse and worse over a few weeks and then turned into pneumonia.

During the late 1800s and early 1900s, pneumonia was the leading cause of death from an infectious disease and the third leading cause of death overall. Time to put on your doctor's coat and not get grossed out: Pneumonia causes the tiny air sacs (alveoli) in your lungs to fill with pus and fluid. If enough of them fill up with fluid, you can have trouble breathing. You may not be able to get enough fresh oxygen from your lungs circulated throughout your body. The medical name for this is respiratory failure. Penicillin, which became the miracle drug for pneumonia, was not used until 1942.

Feeling very sick and weak, Annie wrote one last letter home in which she begged her parents to come get her. The letter reached her parents only days before they received a letter from the school's headmistress saying that Annie had died.

Too late to save her while she was alive, her parents came and took her body home.

For some reason, her spirit decided to stay at the Institute. We don't know if visitors to the area who spent their summers at the former school, then a hotel, experienced Annie's sad spirit. But today tourists tell stories of being surprised, even scared, by an invisible presence that seems to sneak up behind them. Others describe feeling sudden cold spots in the rooms they walk into. Some people have heard mysterious and spooky music or have seen a weird blue light sparkling and dancing in the top-floor windows. A few claim to have seen Annie.

One girl who visited the Patapsco Female Institute Historic Park got separated from her tour group. She described her frightening experience. She was standing in front of the school, deciding which way to go to find the rest of the group she had come to the park with when something caught her eye. Can you guess? She said a young girl wearing a flowing gown walked out of a door, across a porch, and down the stair to the lawn. A that exact moment, the girl in the long dress just disappeared. When the visiting girl tried to find the spirit again, she realized that the porch had vanished, too! Was it all just a dream?

Why do you think Annie's ghost didn't leave when her parents picked up her body? Maybe she didn't know they had come for her. Maybe she is still waiting and waiting . . . Poor Annie!

Did Any-BODY See the Ghosts at Al's BODY Shop?

Sometimes ghosts choose to haunt very ordinary places—not your typical creepy-looking big houses. That seems to be true for an old automobile garage that sits back from the road at 3711 Old Columbia Pike. Built in the 1920s when cars were becoming more popular, the single-story cinder-block garage is listed in the Maryland Inventory of Historic Properties as the Ridgely Building. Maybe part of why spirits gather there is its location near the Ellicott Family Cemetery on the banks of the Tiber River tributary called Cat Rock Run or Wildcat Branch. Over the years, several different businesses have popped up in this modest auto garage. Many of the past and present shop owners and customers talk about their scary and not-so scary encounters with the supernatural. Is there just one visitor from beyond . . . or are we talking about a gaggle of ghosts?

Some long-time residents think the garage was built on top of an old cemetery that was moved. One elderly man who was a child during the Civil War claimed to have seen bodies of Union soldiers temporarily buried there until their families could come and move them. This was after the Battle of Monocacy, fought just outside Frederick, Maryland, on July 9, 1864. This battle isn't the most well known, but was a critical one. It prevented the Confederate Army from attacking Washington, D.C., the Union's capitol.

Called Al's Garage by local folks, its real name was Al's Body Shop. It was owned and operated by Albert Franklin Baer, who was born in April 1960 and died in his garage in April 2001.

Soon after Al's death, the dirty and messy shop was turned into a fancy business called What's in Store, where you could buy modern furniture, unusual lamps, and other decorations for your home. Later on, a local florist set up shop. Sometime later, the place became the Well, a health and wellness center where you could take yoga and dance classes. Now the former auto shop is home to a very different kind of repair business: it's called Ooh La La! Hair Salon, it's where you go to get your hair done.

Many of Al's friends and relatives report that during his life he often saw "people" darting in and out of the shadows in his body shop. Do you think they are the restless, lonely spirits of Civil War soldiers buried under the building?

The encounters with ghosts started when What's in Store first opened. One of the new owners described seeing a man leaning against the wall inside the store. The owner hadn't unlocked the door yet so he worried the store had been broken into. He called out, "Hey,

how did you get in here?" In an instant, the man disappeared.

When he told his business partner about what had happened and described what the man looked like, his partner said the man might have been Al standing where his old desk used to be. Maybe Al's spirit was showing up to make sure work was getting done!

Al seemed to hang around when each new business moved in. The owner of Well yoga center reported how heavy objects, even shelves, would suddenly move on their

own, one time breaking a glass table they fell on. Several yoga students said someone or something tickled their feet during class. When the yoga center was moving out, some students who said they had special powers did a cleansing ritual to drive Al's spirit away, but the magic failed. The manager of Ooh La La! Hair Salon says that since moving in, she's heard faint music from the 1950s playing near the shampooing station, and one time saw a shadowy figure dressed in overalls standing in the corner of the shop. And, most upsetting of all, one day she felt an icy hand touch her legs as she walked out the door. Was this Al's ghost flirting with the young hairdresser, or was this his way of asking, "Hey, how about a shave and a haircut?"

Whatever he was trying to communicate, it seems that Al plans to stay in his Body Shop for eternity—just without his body! And perhaps, the Civil War soldiers left behind help Al stir up some excitement to break the boredom of being ghosts!

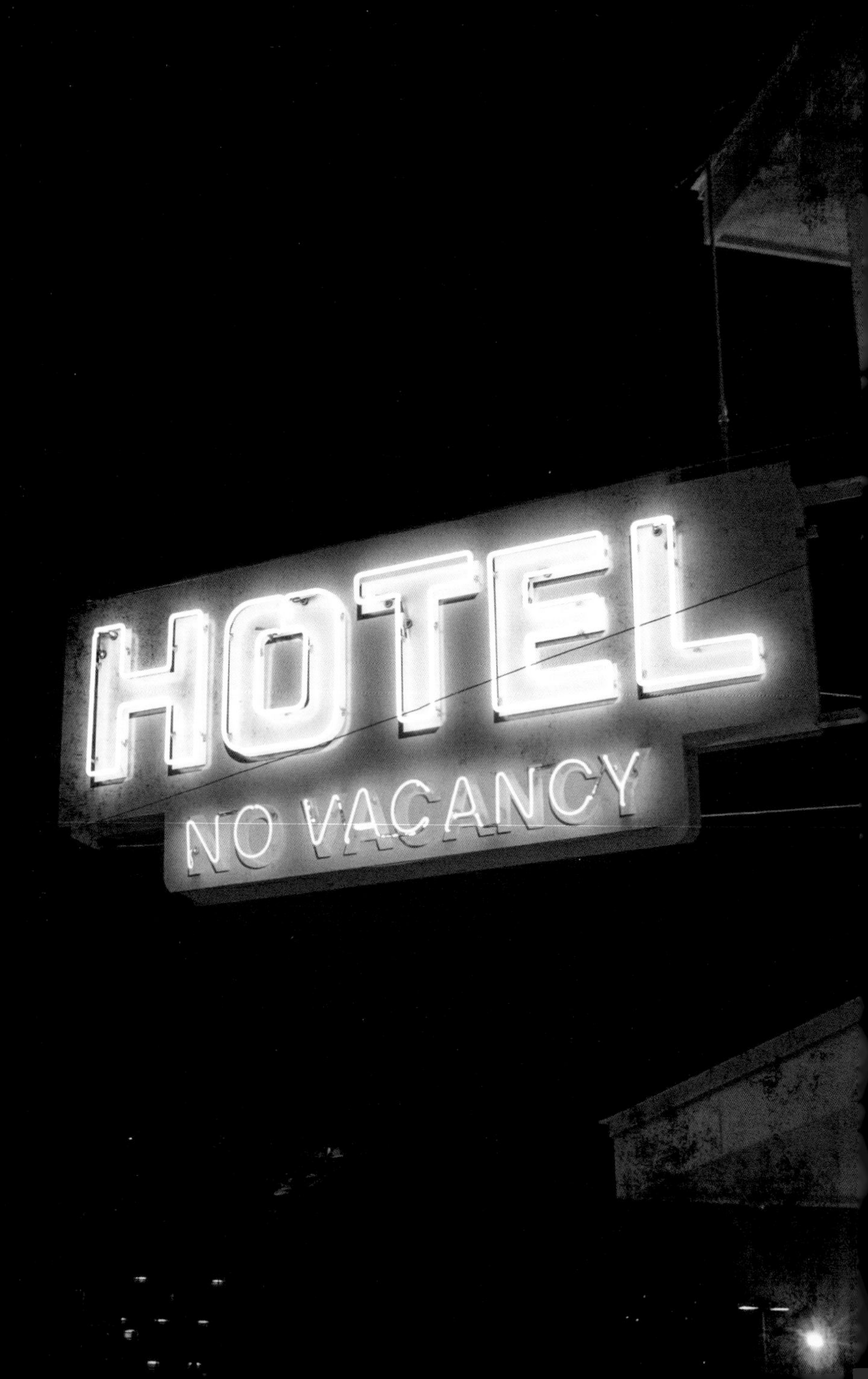
HOTEL
NO VACANCY

CHAPTER 8

The Man Who Wouldn't Check Out

Have you read the novel or seen the movie adaptation of *The Shining*? This famous horror novel, written by Steven King in 1997, is set in an isolated, haunted hotel in the Colorado Rockies. Be warned: That book and movie might give you nightmares! This tale about a haunted hotel in Ellicott City, Maryland, has no mountain views, and would only be a 3 on a 10-point "scare your pants off" scale. But still…there's something about creepy old hotels…

Bad luck seemed to haunt this five-story hotel called The Howard House, which was bought and sold several times over the years since it was built around 1840 at 8282 Main Street. Like most buildings on the north side of Main Street, the hotel was built into a steep slope of living granite so that the third floor of the front elevation is the ground floor for the back of the building. The back of the building faces what is now Church Road, originally called Ellicott Street.

The hotel changed hands many times, but eventually it became successful, a favorite place for visitors to Ellicott's Mills to dine and lodge. The hotel's bar was located on the first floor; the dining room was on the second floor.

In 1882, the town enacted a law forbidding the sale of "spirituous, fermented or intoxicating liquors," forcing the owner to close the hotel bar. In a stroke of genius, the owner added other intoxicating items to the menus, including homemade ice cream, ginger ale, and sarsaparilla, a soft drink similar to root beer. Townspeople would often use The Howard House as a shortcut to get up the hill from Main Street to the courthouse, which encouraged more folks to enjoy the hotel's delicious sweets as they made their way through town.

Over the years, the building also featured several apartments and retail spaces. Many stories are told about the former hotel and apartment guests, including one unfortunate man who didn't want to check out—even after death.

As the story goes, a tenant who lived in an apartment on the top floor of the Howard House was convinced she was sharing the place with a ghost. She came to believe that a previous tenant had never moved out, even though he was no longer alive. She named the spirit "Dennis." The ghostly marvels started as soon as she moved in. She heard odd, unexplainable sounds. Pots and pans clanged in the middle of the night. A male voice whispered words she couldn't understand. Sudden spurts of cold air appeared and disappeared in the living room and kitchen, which caused her cat to flee with his fur standing up and then refuse to go into that part of the apartment. Can you picture that scaredy cat? Would you be scared too?

These mysterious occurrences continued until the woman had to go out of town and asked a friend to stay in the apartment and watch her cat. This friend was known to have skills that allowed her to communicate with spirits, so the woman asked her to find out who "Dennis" was and why he was in the apartment.

When the woman came home, her friend told her she had "talked" to the ghost. She believed he was a young man, a construction worker, who had died on the job when the hotel was being completed in 1850. "Dennis" had fallen through the unfinished roof on the Church Road side of the building and died in the space between her kitchen and living room, exactly where those freezing areas were located. The friend said the young man's spirit wanted to leave but didn't know how.

Two weeks later, an employee at the Howard County Welcome Center who had done some historical research confirmed the story of the accident. After that, the unexplained ghostly phenomena came to an end. The cat calmed down. Apparently, the tenant's friend had been able to help "Dennis" finally check out of the Howard House Hotel.

Another spooky Howard Hotel story involves a resident of Mount Ida, the name of the Ellicott family mansion where well-known businessman Louis Thomas Clark lived with his family. Born in 1871, Clark was in his late fifties when he purchased Radcliffe's Emporium, the stone building on the north side of Main Street next to the Patapsco River, in which he opened a grocery store. For the next thirty years, Clark walked down that road to Main Street and down to his store in the morning and returned home at the end of the day.

The story that has been passed around for decades is this: Mr. Clark was known to visit with neighborhood children on the back porch of the Howard House Hotel to entertain them with stories of early times in that city. On one unforgettable day, Mr. Clark told his stories later than usual that afternoon. After most of the kids had left, just two young boys stayed to visit with Mr. Clark, whom they were very fond of. After a while, Mr. Clark stood up to leave, and said to the boys, "Well, young gentlemen, it's time for me to go." When the children asked when he'd be coming back to tell more stories, he said, "Oh, I don't think I'll be back for quite a while." Then he turned and started walking up Church Road.

No sooner had Mr. Clark disappeared from view, the boys heard the loud wail of an ambulance siren and watched it race up Church Road followed by police cars. Not long after, one of the police cars slowly drove down the hill. The boys flagged down one car and asked what had happened.

"We were just up at Clark's," the police officer explained.

"What happened?" asked the boys. "Mr. Clark just left here a little bit ago. He'd been telling us stories for hours."

"No, that can't be, boys," said the police officer. "Mr. Clark has been dead for over four hours."

Louis Thomas Clark died in Ellicott City on December 3, 1957 and is buried with family members in St. John's Cemetery—perhaps after one last visit to the hotel he loved.

Don't let these stories scare you away from spending a night in a hotel some day: just be sure to check under the bed!

CHAPTER 9

A Ghostly Re-Enactment of a Civil War Soldier's Failed Escape

As you learned in history class, the Civil War in the United States began in 1861, after many years of ongoing disagreements between northern and southern states over slavery, states' rights, and westward expansion. The election of Abraham Lincoln as president in 1860 caused seven southern states to secede, or "formerly withdraw," from the US and form the Confederate States of America; four more states soon joined them. The War Between the States, as the Civil War was called, ended with the Confederate Army's surrender in 1865. The conflict was the costliest and deadliest war ever fought on American soil, with some 620,000 of 2.4 million soldiers killed, millions injured, and much of the South left in ruin.

Perhaps you have traveled to places across the country where memorials have been built to honor the fallen soldiers on both sides of this terrible war. Maybe you have heard about American Civil War re-enactors, regular folks who are sometimes called "living historians," who dress up in period costumes and harmlessly (but accurately) stage a particular battle or other event associated with the American Civil War.

And then there are ghostly re-enactments, such as this chilling story. During the Civil War, Maryland was a border state. Although it was a slave state, it never seceded from the Union. Throughout the course of the war, about 80,000 Marylanders served in Union armies, compared to about 20,000 who served in the Confederate armies.

The story goes that on this one dreadful night, a young Confederate soldier escaped from the custody of Union troops that were guarding captured soldiers at the Thomas Viaduct in Elkridge. Somehow he managed to sneak away and disappear into the dark woods of what is now the Patapsco State Park. By the time he reached the railroad tracks, he was lost and confused. So he decided to follow the tracks, hoping that they led south toward Washington, D.C., and back toward his home. Tragically, that five-mile route took him straight into Ellicott City. He realized his mistake when he recognized the lights of the town from which he'd been captured.

The Confederate soldier had good reason to be scared out of his wits. Ellicott City was home to the Patapsco Guard and a provost marshal, a title given to a person in charge of military police. This meant that there were Union soldiers everywhere. Fearfully, he crept along Maryland Avenue near the B&O Railroad Station's freight house and ran down Tiber Alley. He snuck across Main Street and ran up the long flight of stairs next to the Railroad Hotel, hoping to find a closet in which to hide. Unfortunately, his plan failed. The Union soldiers in Elkridge had telegraphed a warning about their escaped prisoner. By the time the young soldier reached Ellicott City, he was a wanted man. The Union soldiers didn't have to search for long because many of the Patapsco Guard were bunking at the Railroad Hotel. Talk about choosing the worst place to hide! Witnesses at the time say the young man reached the third floor of the hotel, where two Union soldiers saw him. Scared to death, he turned around and started running down the same steps he had just come up, hoping he could escape and run into the woods along the train tracks as he'd done in Elkridge.

He'd just started down the stairs when one of the Union soldiers took aim and shot him in the back. The force of the bullet caused him to tumble head over heels down the steep steps. By the time the two soldiers reached him, he was dead. Killings are a part of war, but the fact that he was shot, not on a battlefield, but inside a hotel, makes the act seem like murder.

The brutality of the young soldier's death may be what caused his spirit to be imprisoned for eternity and for his death to be replayed on moonless nights ever since. Over many decades, witnesses say they feel the presence of the young soldier on the third floor of the hotel, and some insist they have heard the pounding sound of running feet as he tries, again and again, to escape. Paranormal investigators, a fancy term for "ghost hunters," report they have detected motion on the steps leading up to the third floor. And a few insist they have seen the phantom of a Confederate soldier running for dear life down the steep outdoor stairway between the Railroad Hotel and the Town Hall. It appears there is no escape for a runaway Civil War prisoner. The unlucky young man's spirit is trapped for all time in Ellicott City's Railroad Hotel, where some guests check in but never check out!

The Odd Fellow
Who Turned into
a Ghost Fellow

Here's a bittersweet tale that illustrates how it may be possible to be a good person even after one's life has ended. Some might argue that this strange story illustrates the true meaning of *community spirit*.

The story takes place in a striking stone building located at 8134 Main Street. It is home to one of Ellicott City's oldest charitable social organizations—the Independent Order of Odd Fellows Centre Lodge No. 40.

Built in the mid 1800s, the lodge is one of the oldest buildings on this side of town. It was a harness shop until 1860, when the new owners, the Mercer family, sold the building to the Odd Fellows. The Elliot City branch of this charitable organization was launched in 1843, but the group was founded in eighteenth-century England by community-minded men, women, and young people, who shared a belief in a supreme being and that friendship, love, and truth are the basic guidelines that people should follow every day. Why was it called Odd Fellows? It seems that when the order was created, it was "deemed odd" to find people organized to unselfishly care for those in need and work to benefit all of mankind. The world today could certainly benefit from more odd people like these, don't you agree?

Until the late 1970s, a sign featuring three links of chain with the letters F, L, and T, symbolizing the order's ideals of Friendship, Love, and Truth, was displayed on the front of the building between the second and third floors. Odd Fellows meetings have taken place in the lodge's third-floor hall since 1863. The second floor is rented out as apartments. Over the years many different shops have occupied rooms on the first floor.

Although the Centre Lodge has been part of the Ellicott City community for more than 150 years, the ghost that haunts the building is a newcomer. In the 1970s, the lodge inducted a young man named Tom, the son of one of its members. He accepted his membership with great enthusiasm. To show how much he appreciated being part of this group, Tom enthusiastically volunteered to set up the hall for the order's Thursday night meetings. He would arrive early, set up the tables and chairs, and then stand at the top of the steep stairs to greet members as they arrived. He happily took on this responsibility every week, never missing a meeting. But life had a different plan for Tom. One night, while he was driving back to Ellicott City from western Howard County,

his car was struck by another vehicle that came speeding around a bend directly into Tom's lane. Tom was killed instantly.

When the lodge members heard about the accident, they immediately cancelled their next weekly meeting out of respect for the young man. However, the more they thought about it, they decided that Tom would have wanted them to continue the work of the organization. So they decided to go forward with the weekly meeting. A few members agreed to arrive early, knowing that Tom wouldn't be there to set things up.

But when the members walked up the stairs and opened the door to the meeting room, they stood in stunned silence. What they saw shocked them. All the tables and chairs were in their rightful place, and the materials for the meeting were at each member's place. How was this possible? Some thought a member had arrived early to do this. Others believe that Tom's kindness wasn't limited by death and that his spirit had done this good deed for the members whose work he so admired. Although his precious life was snuffed out in the disastrous car accident, death was no match for his dedication.

The Odd Fellows still continue to meet in the hall on the top floor of the building. Tenants who live in the apartments below the meeting space report hearing and seeing odd things, decades after Tom's tragic death. Witnesses claim that exactly half an hour before members are due to arrive, they hear footsteps above and sounds of chairs moving across the old wooden floor above them. When these strange sounds first occurred, one of the tenants ran upstairs to see who was making all this noise. But they found no one. Mysteriously, the room was set up for the meeting! Amazing, right? So now, every Thursday, folks who live in the building accept that there is nothing really odd about it: Tom's ghostly existence is responsible for the room being prepared for the meetings he so cherished in his short life.

CHAPTER 11

A Staring Contest You Won't Win

In the paranormal world, a "portal" is believed to be an invisible passage into another plane of existence. Sometimes ghosts—friendly and not so friendly—travel back and forth through portals that are often located near bridges or inside tunnels. This scary tale warns that an evil spirit hangs out inside an Ellicott City tunnel. This is one ghost you definitely don't want to meet.

Close by the hills of College Avenue and what used to be St. Mary's Seminary is a portal that lets trains travel between Baltimore and Ellicott City. It is drilled into a cliff on the banks of the rushing river below. The Ilchester Tunnel is like a magnet, drawing people who are attracted to danger to stare into the darkness of the tunnel, hoping to catch a glimpse of a nasty spirit that won't let them look away.

The Ilchester Tunnel, 1,405 feet long, is the second longest tunnel on the Baltimore & Ohio Railroad's Old Main Line. Built around 1900 to go around a sharp curve in the road first used by horse-drawn carriages, the tunnel reached from Baltimore to Ellicott's Mills. The tunnel and a replacement bridge were built about four hundred feet upstream from an earlier structure which had been partially destroyed in the great flood of 1868.

The legend of the "Blink Man" started in the 1920s, or earlier. During the Great Depression, a terrible worldwide situation that started in the United States in which hundreds of thousands of people lost their jobs and homes, many desperate people hopped on trains to travel to other towns, in the hope of finding work. These people were called hoboes.

This story tells of an old hobo walking through the tunnel around midnight one evening when he was killed by a speeding train. It is believed that the violent way he died caused his spirit to be trapped in the tunnel. The miserable ghoul lives in the dark emptiness, just waiting to scare to death anyone foolish or brave enough to try to stare him down.

Please don't try this yourself, but the story goes that if you stand on the Howard County side of the railroad bridge at exactly 11:00 p.m. and stare into the Ilchester Tunnel without blinking for one full hour, you will experience a one-way trip that you won't live to tell your friends about.

At exactly midnight, the Blink Man will suddenly appear at the far end of the tunnel.

He doesn't stay there. When the curious person blinks after seeing the ghost, it moves closer and closer, each time the person blinks. This goes on until the Blink Man is almost touching the person's face. That's when the worst part begins as the victim feels the ghost's long eyelashes flutter against his or her face.

Usually, these gentle touches with people we know and love are very pleasant and are called "butterfly kisses." But with this nasty ghost, the eyelashes can cause someone to go crazy on the spot. Some victims become deranged and pull out their own eyes in a fit of uncontrollable anger and fear. Other stories say that when victims see the Blink man getting closer and closer, they are simply scared to death and immediately fall down dead of a heart attack.

Way back in the sixteenth century, a German alchemist named Jakob Bohme called these kinds of encounters "Flimmern-Geist," which means "flicker-ghost or spirit." The belief is that these paranormal beings have died violently and spend eternity just out of sight of the living. Some people believe the Ilchester Tunnel is a portal, or an "interdimensional focal point" where the world of the living meets the spiritual world. If you are in one of these focal points and your stare into the darkness, you invite invisible ghosts to show up. When they do, if you don't look away, you will be frozen in place . . . forever.

This story doesn't have a happy ending. It is believed that no one has ever survived a meeting with the Blink Man. It can't be proved for certain whether people who have seen the spirit died from pulling out their own eyes, were scared to death, or didn't get out of the way of a speeding train. But it's probably a good idea to never, ever, gaze into this or any dark tunnel, hoping for a staring contest that you are certain to lose.

Deborah Morgenthal is a freelance writer and editor. As former Editorial Director at Lark Books, she wrote and edited dozens of books about "making stuff" for grown-ups and kids. When she's not writing and editing, she can be found out hiking with her wonder dog, Maisie.

Check out some of the other Spooky America titles available now!

Spooky America was adapted from the creeptastic Haunted America series for adults. Haunted America explores historical haunts in cities and regions across America. Each book chronicles both the widely known and less-familiar history behind local ghosts and other unexplained mysteries. Here's more from *Haunted Ellicott City* author Shelley Davies Wygant:

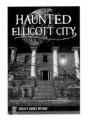